Boost Your Income Working Online At Home

Written by a Work at Home Mum

-by-

Stephanie Law

I0470944

First Edition, April 2013

Copyright 2013, by Stephanie Law

One year ago I decided I was leaving the rat race behind. I wanted to work from home, be my own boss and, most importantly, spend quality time with my family.

It has not been easy finding work from home, but among the scams and low paying jobs I have found some legitimate work at home opportunities that any stay-at-home parent, or indeed anyone who needs a financial boost, can have a go at. From reviewing music, writing hotel descriptions, designing t-shirts, evaluating web sites and answering questions, there is something for everyone here to make money with. With some hard work and dedication you can really increase your income and enjoy working from home.

The opportunities I have listed in this ebook are totally legitimate. These are websites that I myself personally use and continue to use on a daily/weekly basis. These are genuine ways to boost your income and, most importantly, they do not involve you paying any money in any way, shape or form at any stage!

I am not a writer by trade, nor a salesperson. I am not a scam artist trying to make money. I am a Mummy, pure and simple. I wanted to work online from home to make more money whilst also bringing up my family.

When I first started out on my journey to become a work from home Mummy, I found an abundance of information on how to work online from home. It was a total minefield and I quickly became overcome with the enormity of what I was trying to achieve. Initially, I had no idea where to start looking for work online and so I did what anyone else would do – I carried out basic searches on Google (other search engines are available) to see what I could find. I can safely say that it has taken me the best part of a year to filter out the legitimate work at home jobs from the scams that are floating around the internet.

And that is why I have written this ebook. After all the time I have spent researching online, I decided to give a little back and share the information that I have found with you.

I hope that you enjoy reading my first ebook and that what I have found in my quest to make money online will help you to do the very same. Good luck, and enjoy!

Table of Contents

1.   **Review Music Tracks**

Do you love listening to music? Would you love to be able to review up and coming artists and tracks before they are released? Well guess what? Now you can - and you can get PAID for this too!

Slice the Pie is a great site that I have found in my never ending quest to make money online from home. After you have taken a few minutes to quickly register on their site, Slice the Pie will ask you to confirm what sort of music you like to listen to. You will be asked, for example, if you like to listen to Classical, Rock, Pop, Dance music and many more. This is to make sure that Slice the Pie will only ask you to review tracks relating to the genre(s) of music that you actually enjoy listening to, which makes it even easier for you to make money!

It is so easy to get started reviewing tracks on Slice the Pie. As soon as you sign into your account you will see a small box and the music will start to play immediately. In this small box you are then asked to type your review of the track that you can hear playing. You can start to type this review as soon as the music plays, which really helps a lot as this means you don't have to remember everything you thought of that particular track as it was being played to you. I always like to say something about the introduction to the track along with how the vocals matched it, or didn't as the case may be. Slice the Pie really want you to be honest about the music tracks you are reviewing, so don't worry about leaving a negative review - you will not be penalised at all for this and you will still earn money! Make sure and be as descriptive as you can in your review and comment on the lyrics, melody, the artist's voice and anything else that you did or did not like.

Your reviews on Slice the Pie will go back to the unsigned artists to help them improve their tracks, so it is really important that you give constructive criticism, or explain what you liked so much about the track so that the artist can use your feedback. As a reward for this, Slice the Pie will pay you, and the longer, more well written and descriptive your reviews are, the more money you will earn for that review.

Slice the Pie pay out when your account reaches $10 via Paypal and I have found this really easy to achieve.

If you are interested in reviewing music tracks for money, or would just like to find out some more information, then visit www.slicethepie.com

2.   **Write Hotel Descriptions**

Trivago.co.uk is a hotel price comparison website which compares prices of over 150 hotels. Whenever a new hotel is submitted to Trivago for inclusion on their website, freelancers like you and me can earn money by writing a description of that hotel to help people who subsequently wish to make a booking at that particular hotel.

Please note that this freelance opportunity is for writing hotel descriptions and not reviews, so it is not a requirement that you have had to visit these hotels at all. You can simply do a quick bit of research online to find out information about the hotel and form your description around it.

For each hotel description that you write you will earn €1 plus Trivago miles which can be changed into money.

Here is a step by step guide on how to get started writing hotel descriptions with Trivago today:

1.   Register a free account on www.trivago.co.uk
2.   Send a short email to info@trivago.co.uk asking to join the Descriptions Team;

3.   Once approved, start writing descriptions and earning money!

Your descriptions are not a review of the hotel and as such should be neutral in context. You should start your description by stating the hotel's name and then describe the location, nearby tourist attractions, hotel type and facilities etc. Your hotel description should be between 1000 to 1200 characters (not words) in length. Once submitted, your description will be proof read and checked by an editor before it is published live on the Trivago website.

I found it really fun writing these hotel descriptions and I love seeing my descriptions there in black and white on the Trivago website for everyone to see. There is also a great community of people on Trivago to help you on the way if you need assistance.

For more information on how to start writing your own hotel descriptions check out:

http://www.trivago.co.uk/static.php?&sid=2116&tld=uk and http://www.trivago.co.uk/help.php?sid=263

3.   Write short articles and evaluate web searches

Clickworker is a great site that I was really excited to find. This site was recommended by a poster on a forum that I regularly read and I have been earning money with Clickworker ever since.

Clickworker is a site that uses freelancers who work from their own computers to carry out digital tasks. These tasks can range from evaluating web search results, to writing short articles and advertisements. You decide what tasks you want to complete and how many. When you log into your account you will easily see the jobs that are available and how much you will be paid for doing them, so you know upfront exactly how much you are going to earn. As you progress and do more and more tasks, you will see the amount you are earning increasing at the top of the screen which is a great incentive to keep you motivated!

To use Clickworker you do not have to be a skilled writer at all. As I stated in the introduction to this ebook, I am not a writer, yet I make considerable money working for Clickworker.

When you first sign up for a Clickworker account you will be asked to complete some short assessments which will test your grammar, punctuation and spelling. These are relatively simple tasks. It is very important that you score as highly as you can, as this means you will be eligible to take part in more tasks and article writing jobs which means that you will be able to earn more money.

The main tasks that I have carried out on Clickworker are advertisements and articles which are around 250 words in length. Clickworker will explain exactly what you have to do for each writing piece and they provide a very handy list of guidelines that you must stick to. They will tell you what you must include in each piece and how it should be set out. They also have a spellcheck on the page where you type the advertisement/article so that you don't make any mistakes, along with a word count to make sure you have enough of them in there.

The web search evaluation work is very straightforward and easy to complete too. Clickworker will simply show you a screen split into two. On the left hand side will be the term that they searched for online, for example "mechanic Manchester". Below this it will show you the details for a particular business that appeared in that search. On the right hand side you will have to tick "Yes" or "No" to various questions on how relevant the result was to the search. It really is as simple as that!

These are just two of the tasks available through Clickworker but once you sign up and complete your assessments you will see all the work available to you and tasks they have to offer.

Due to confidentiality issues, I cannot reveal more information on the work that I do for Clickworker than this, but trust me, if you have a good grasp of the English language then you will be able to make money with Clickworker.

I have found Clickworker to be a really great source of income and I love the fact that I am paid directly into my Paypal account. As long as there is work available, you can do as many or as little jobs as you like and there is no pressure from Clickworker for you to work a set number of hours at all. It is a totally flexible working position and if I can do it then so can you!

For more information check out www.Clickworker.com

4.   Fill in Market Research Surveys

Ok, so I have included a chapter on filling in surveys online as although not all survey sites generally pay out in cash, they are still a great way to earn an extra income. The survey sites that I use pay out in the way of cash or vouchers, which can then be used either online or instore. These vouchers can usually be redeemed at a variety of stores, so check to make sure you would actually use the vouchers earned at these stores before signing up.

I love filling in surveys for these two market research websites that I am about to tell you about. Why? Because they take so little time out of my day to do (I usually complete them at night in front of the TV) and at the end of the year I use my vouchers earned to pay for my Christmas presents for friends and family! I have been doing these survey sites now for around two years and honestly, it is a great way of saving money at the most expensive time of year. So that is why, although this is not a way of earning money specifically, I have included this section on survey sites, because these vouchers earned will actually save you spending your own money, be it on gifts for loved ones or just a treat for yourself!

So, here are the two survey sites that I use at the moment. I have tried various others which I have come to the conclusion are just not worth my time, and so I will not waste your time with them either.

Some of the surveys that I have received from those companies (who shall remain nameless) have been rather tedious and have seemed to involved too much of my time for the pay that I would get. So, the two survey sites I recommend are:

Valued Opinions

This is my favourite survey website.

Basically, as you would expect, after you sign up to Valued Opinions you will be asked to fill out some profile surveys. It is very important that you fill in all of these surveys and make sure that you are honest with your answers. This will mean that any surveys you will be sent from Valued Opinions will be of interest and relevance to you personally. So, if you don't like watching sport on TV, then say so in your profile survey otherwise you will be sent surveys that are not relevant or interesting to you.

I usually receive one to two surveys per day from Valued Opinions, but I do not qualify for all of the surveys that I am sent. Sometimes they will have reached the desired number of applicants for my age/area etc and you will be screened out, but this doesn't happen all that often.

With Valued Opinions you can cash out once you reach £10 and I have reached this amount relatively quickly in the past. Here is a complete list of all the gift vouchers you can earn through Valued Opinions (remember, you can cash out when you reach just £10): Marks and Spencer; Amazon; Boots; Argos; John Lewis; Marriott Hotels; Dorothy Perkins; Evans; Outfit; Topshop/Topman; Miss Selfridge; Wallis; Burton; Sainsburys; Eventim; Wow; and iTunes. That's a lot of different places for you for spend your well earned vouchers!

To find out more about Valued Opinions, go to www.valuedopinions.co.uk

Global Test Market

Global Test Market is another survey site that I have recently (just this week, actually) signed up to. Again, I had a lot of profile questions to answer to make sure that I am sent the most relevant surveys, but I had them completed quite quickly indeed. I have already been asked to complete six surveys, of which I was screened out of two.

I really like the feel and ease of use of the surveys that I have received so far with Global Test Market. It is early days yet, but I think I am going to be able to cash out very quickly with them too.

The thing I like about Global Test Market is that they pay out in cash as well as vouchers, so you can actually choose which you want. If you choose to be paid in cash, then you can do this via cheque or Paypal. Alternatively, you can redeem your points for gift vouchers, which at the moment are available to spend at Amazon, Homebase or Debenhams.

To sign up with Global Test Market, go to www.globaltestmarket.com and click on "Get Started".

5. **Answer and Ask Questions**

WebAnswers is a questions and answers website where members of the public, along with members of WebAnswers itself, pose questions to be answered. There are many, many categories of questions on WebAnswers from family, finance, work, food and drink and entertainment to name but a few.

In order to get started earning money with WebAnswers, you will firstly need to answer fifty questions. These fifty questions are, if you like, a test to see how good your grammar, punctuation and spelling is. The longer your answers, the better your quality score will be and once you have successfully answered these fifty questions, you will be asked to either create a Google Adsense account, or link your existing account to your WebAnswers account. This is how you will ultimately get paid – by Google Adsense (when you reach the minimum payment threshold, which in the UK is £60).

The idea behind WebAnswers is really simple: answer as many questions as you can and the more you answer, the more you will get paid. If you are "awarded" a winning answer to a question, that is that the person asking the question thinks that you answered it the best, then you will earn revenue from that question for the next year. If the question remains unanswered, then everyone who answered it will share the revenue.

I must emphasise though that it is very important to answer questions that allow you to type a good two to three paragraphs, and that the spelling, punctuation and grammar is 100% perfect. The longer your answer, the higher your quality score, so try not to answer those questions that only require a one word or one sentence answer (for example "What is your favourite colour?"). Those questions are pointless and will only serve to lower your quality score and how much money you will ultimately earn.

I have found it really easy to get started on WebAnswers and the site as a whole is really easy to navigate and work your way around. There is a great sense of community and other members are always ready to offer help and advice if you need it. WebAnswers really is a great way to make money online!

To find out more check out www.webanswers.com and www.google.co.uk/adsense

6. **Sell your Photographs**

Do you have lots of photographs of holidays, people, places and objects clogging up your hard drive? You do? Well then you may just be able to make money selling your photos online!

As yet, I have not personally got around to using this method of making money from my photos, but I have heard some really good things about selling photographs online. I cannot even get my holiday snaps organised in a timely fashion, but when I do I will be selling some of the landscape ones and hopefully making some money from them.

Just spend some time sifting through your pictures and choose the best ones to upload. As with any site, make sure and read the terms and conditions before uploading your pictures and that you are happy with the commission. There are lots of sites like this around out there, so do some research and see what you can find out. This is a really exciting way of making money! Also, check out the next section on Zazzle, as you can make money from your photographs on their site by making canvas and photo prints from your snaps.

Here is a small selection of the websites that I have found where you can upload and sell your photographs:

http://www.alamy.com

http://www.britishimages.co.uk/

http://www.deviantart.com

http://www.fotolia.co.uk

http://www.istockphoto.com

http://www.photobucket.com

http://www.photographersdirect.com

http://www.smugmug.com

7.   **Design Clothing for Money (no skills required!)**

Fancy yourself as a graphic designer but don't know how to go about it? Maybe you have a great eye for detail and design? Now it's time to get your creative juices flowing! Imagine being able to design and sell t-shirts, bags and canvas prints without actually holding any of the physical products? All you have to do is create the items and then sit back and wait on your commission!

Zazzle is a website which sells all manner of items that can be printed with various designs. You can choose from invitations, t-shirts, tote bags, hoodies, caps and many more. All you have to do is create an account and choose an item to design. For example, if you just want to design a simple t-shirt then you just choose the t-shirt you want (these come in various styles for men and women) and insert the text. You can choose the font and colour too. It really is as easy as that – just click, type and sell!

When someone places an order for your design, Zazzle takes care of the printing and shipping and pay you a commission (which you will set yourself at the design stage) for the sale. It's as simple as that!

If you have any photographs that you think would make good wall art, then these can also be uploaded and you can create canvas and poster prints with these too.

Zazzle is a really easy site to use. I am not a graphic designer and I could use it quite simply, so you can too! I created my own Zazzle account and started designing t-shirts and hoodies a few months ago. I am pleased to say that I have already sold several of these items in various sizes and colours. There is nothing as satisfying and exciting as receiving an email from Zazzle letting you know that one of your items has sold and someone is walking around in one of your designs!

I am aiming in the coming weeks to really scale up the number of items that I have for sale on Zazzle. It really took very little effort on my part to start designing my t-shirts and hoodies and I know that if I really knuckled down and applied myself that I could make some serious income with Zazzle. All I need now is some inspiration!

Another website similar to Zazzle that I have heard of is Cafepress. I know that Cafepress works along the same lines as Zazzle and is a reputable site, but I personally have not used them. However, if Zazzle is something that you might be interested in, then you could also look into Cafepress too.

Check out www.zazzle.co.uk and www.cafepress.co.uk

8.   **Create T-Shirt Slogans**

I stumbled across Shot Dead in the Head quite by accident, when I was doing some research on Zazzle. In fact, Shot Dead in the Head is very similar to Zazzle.

Shot Dead in the Head are a t-shirt printing company who are always on the lookout for new designs and slogans for their shirts. If you have a good slogan or idea for a t-shirt then all you have to do is drop them an email with your idea and if they don't already have it for sale and think it has good potential, then they will send you a contract to sign, they will then design a t-shirt around your slogan/idea, and all you have to do is wait for the commissions to roll in!

I haven't as yet tried Shot Dead in the Head, but I have read some good things about them and hopefully I may come up with some ideas that I might put their way. The other thing is, if Shot Dead in the Head don't think your idea is something that they are looking for, then you could simply take your design and make your own shirt, hoodies and bags with it on Zazzle!

Take a look at their website to get a feel for the sort of things that they are looking for and get thinking! www.shotdeadinthehead.com

9.   Fiverr & FiveSquids

Just in case you haven't heard of it, Fiverr is a site based in the US which allows users to post gigs for sale. These gigs could be anything from website design or writing articles to selling earrings and postcards. You decide what you can offer, and simply post your gig up for sale for $5 (hence the name Fiverr).

Get your thinking cap on. What can you do for a fiver? Do some typing? Make a YouTube video? Send a postcard? Whatever it is, make sure it is something that you can turn around quickly. The more you can do, the more money you will make!

A lot of people make money from posting gigs on Fiverr and make a good living out of it. Don't be put off by the fact that there are a lot of people on there - just find something that you are good at and put it up for sale. The UK version of Fiverr is called FiveSquids, but don't limit yourself to just one of these sites, sign up for both and you will have double the success! It takes only a few minutes to sign up to both of these sites and start selling, so go on, get to it!

Also check out the wanted lists on each of these sites. You will find people who want someone to do a particular task and hopefully you will be able to help them out! Check out www.fiverr.com and www.fivesquids.co.uk

10.   Audio Typing Online

As an audio typist by trade, I have found several online companies that outsource audio typing to transcriptionists who work from home. You need to be an experienced audio typist to carry out this work as these companies demand a very high standard of work and if you don't produce good quality work then you could have your contract terminated.

A quick Google search for "audio transcription companies" or "audio typists required" will bring up lots of results, which you can then narrow down by country if need be. There are simply too many to list here in this ebook! Once you have found a company you may be interested in working for (this will most likely be on a self employed basis) then do a quick search on the internet to see if you can find a review from someone who has worked for them.

I will however single out one particular company that I have recently come across and that is TranscribeMe.

TranscribeMe outsource their audio transcription work to audio typists who work from home. You simply sign up, pass a short test and then you can begin working. I am mentioning this company in particular as you work on their own system, which means you don't have to download any software or audio yourself to your computer, nor do you need a footpedal as the audio itself is just controlled onscreen by your mouse. All you have to do is log onto their system and type what you hear.

I am in the early stages of working for TranscribeMe, but so far I like what I see. On your screen you will see a box at the left hand side where you can play, fast forward or rewind the audio using your mouse and a small box for you to type the actual transcription. On the right hand side you will see the guidelines for how to lay out your transcription. It is important that you set your transcription out exactly as TranscribeMe ask, or you may not get paid!

What I particularly like about TranscribeMe is that the audio recordings are relatively short in length - usually around ten seconds or so - which means that if I get interrupted that I am not losing my way in a long piece of audio. It gives me even more flexibility to work when I want and for how long I want.

You can find out more about TranscribeMe here: www.transcribeme.com

Also check out the next section for freelance websites that also offer work for audio typists.

11.   Become a Freelancer

Do you have a particular skill, such as audio typing, web design or article writing? Could you become a Virtual Assistant working from home? Then freelancing is something that may fit in around your family life.

As a freelancer you will have the freedom to work when you want, for how long you want. Sites such as People Per Hour, Elance and Odesk have a wide range of freelance jobs available for every skill set.

Once you register on any of these websites, you will be asked to complete your profile. Your profile is extremely important and will be one of the first things that a prospective client will look at before awarding you a job.

Here are my top tips for filling out your profile:

1. Put in as much relevant information as you possibly can. Don't overload your profile with information that prospective clients don't need to know. Simply state what you can do and your expertise in that particular area.

2. Upload your CV - again, keep the information in this relevant and keep it to only one or two pages at most.

3.   Upload a photograph of yourself. Clients like to see who they are potentially going to work with and sometimes a photograph rather than a logo, makes you seem more personal to a prospective client. Don't however use a holiday or family snap - you want to come across as a professional individual who takes their work seriously. I have actually come across some terrible photographs of freelancers, including one Virtual Assistant whose picture was of her having a very merry time at her Christmas party!

4.   Upload examples of your work. If you are a website designer, then point prospective clients to websites you have designed. If are a typist, upload documents you have typed (whilst also removing any sensitive or confidential information).

5.   Proof read your entire profile and CV making sure there are no spelling, punctuation or grammatical errors - you don't want to put a client off by a silly typing error.

6.   Upload any references that you have from previous, relevant employers/clients.

I recommend only applying for freelance jobs once you have successfully completed all of the above steps. The first thing a potential client is going to do is to check your profile. The more professional and complete profile you have, the better chance you have of securing work for yourself and starting your freelance career!

It can of course be very difficult to start winning jobs on freelance websites as you will be competing against other freelancers who have been working for those sites for a long period of time. Do not be put off by this. Instead you may find that your best course of action is to submit a low bid for your first few jobs. I know that this will feel like you are potentially working for nothing, but if you can secure a few jobs by submitting the lowest bid, do the work to the best of your ability, and then ask the client to submit references onto your profile, then this will stand you in good stead for the next potential high paying client. Now you will have some glowing references that stand out on your profile for your next clients to see and you can price your jobs at the rate you usually would. Think of this process as a means to an end and you will be glad that you did!

Check out www.peopleperhour.com www.odesk.com and www.elance.com

12. Use Ebay to Make Even More Money

Okay, so everyone has heard of Ebay for buying and selling. I'm hoping that if you are reading this that you have already sold all that junk lying about your house and made money from it (if not, why not?).

I have two other suggestions for you in relation to making money with Ebay.

Firstly, check out your local charity shops and car boot sales and see what bargains you can find. I personally know people who have found designer clothing in their local charity shops that they have bought for only a couple of pounds, to then sell them on Ebay for a lot more money! Designer handbags and vintage jewellery can also be good sellers. Make sure and check out Ebay before you visit the charity shops and car boot sales to get a feel for what will and won't sell - the completed listings section on the left hand side will tell you what the final selling prices were. Or even better, if you have a smartphone, then use this when you are in the shop to find out!

The second way to make money with Ebay is to offer to sell other people's stuff on Ebay - people who aren't internet savvy, or don't have an Ebay account. You could offer to do this and keep a certain percentage of the final selling price. Don't forget to take listing fees, final selling fees and Paypal fees into account also. If you were very confident in doing this for your friends and family then you could progress to putting an advert in your local paper or online (Gumtree and Facebook for example) offering the same service. Or why not offer to create Ebay and Paypal accounts for these people and show them how to do it themselves? You could easily charge an hourly or flat rate for this service. Remember, what you think is something very easy to do, may seem really daunting and difficult for someone use. Use this to your advantage!

13.　　　Create Facebook Pages or Websites for your Local Businesses

Local businesses can be a great source of income for you. Look around your local shops and businesses and ask yourself if you think they have a website or a Facebook page. Make a quick list of the businesses that you can see and do some research when you get home. Many of these businesses don't have the know how or even the time to create an online presence and this is where you come in!

Lots of us have Facebook pages so who better to create Facebook pages for local businesses than you? If you run your own Facebook account then you know what you are doing and you can offer this service to people in your local area who don't know how to do this. Remember what I have said previously: what may seem like something very simple to you can seem very daunting and difficult to those who don't know how to do it.

You could easily offer to create Facebook pages for local businesses for anywhere between £50 and £100 per page. You could also offer to manage it for that said business, posting deals and exciting news for them each week and connecting with local people and other businesses. If you have experience of creating websites then you could offer this service too.

Take a look around and see how many businesses you could offer this service to in your area and you could soon be making money from something you are good at and know a lot about, by working from home!

14.   And Finally,

Thank you for taking the time to purchase and read my first ever ebook. I hope that the online job opportunities that I have found and shared with you help you on your quest to boost your income working online at home.

It can take dedication and hard work, and sometimes to be able to think outside the box, but just like me, you can start working online at home today, with no outlay, and hopefully become successful at it too.

If you enjoyed reading this ebook then I would be eternally grateful if you would leave me some feedback on Amazon and then some day soon (when I am brave enough to pluck up the courage!) I will read your comments. Until next time...

Thank You,

Stephanie Law